STRESS-
PROOF
YOUR TEEN

STRESS-PROOF YOUR TEEN

Helping Your Teen Manage Stress and Build Healthy Habits

HEATH DINGWELL, PH. D.

TURNER

Turner Publishing Company

200 4th Avenue North • Suite 950
Nashville, Tennessee 37219

445 Park Avenue • 9th Floor
New York, NY 10022

www.turnerpublishing.com

Stress-Proof Your Teen:
Helping Your Teen Manage Stress and Build Healthy Habits

This book is also available in gift book format as
46 Things You Can Do To Help Your Teen Manage Stress (978-1-59652-741-6)

This book is meant for discussion purposes only. Before taking any action related
to your child's mental or physical health, you should seek the advice of a medical
or healthcare professional.

Cover design by Mike Penticost

Library of Congress Cataloging-in-Publication Data

Dingwell, Heath.
Stress-proof your teen : helping your teen manage stress and build healthy
habits / Heath Dingwell.
    p. cm.
Includes bibliographical references.
ISBN 978-1-59652-823-9
1. Stress management for teenagers. 2. Stress in adolescence. I. Title.
BF724.3.S86D563 2011
649'.125--dc22

                          2011007470

Printed in the United States of America
11 12 13 14 15 16 17—0 9 8 7 6 5 4 3 2

People are always blaming their circumstances for what they are. I don't believe in circumstances. The people who get on in this world are the people who get up and look for the circumstances they want, and, if they can't find them, make them.

~ George Bernard Shaw

Contents

Introduction

Stress is a natural part of life. It is said that the only time you don't experience stress is when you're dead. That's not too comforting if you have a difficult time dealing with life's stresses.

As I'm sure you remember, the teenage years can be especially stressful. The body is going through physical changes. Hormones are raging. Peer pressure tends to be at an all-time high. Older teenagers have to start deciding whether they want to go to college, a technical-vocational school, or straight into the workforce. Family finances may weigh on them. And the list goes on.

Because you are reading this, I assume you are a concerned parent. Parents can help their teenagers find ways to better manage stress. This book will help provide you with a better understanding of the causes of teenage stress, common reactions, and how to help your teen cope. Consider this book as a resource or reference guide instead of something you need to read from cover to cover. That said, it certainly won't hurt to read all of the chapters, since they may help you realize your teen is experiencing stress that you have not noticed.

If nothing else, it is important for you to read the chapters on listening, asking how to get help, and suspending judgment. If you don't communicate with your teenager about his life, then you won't be able to do the best job possible helping him deal with the stress. If you don't temporarily take a step back and try to look at things through his eyes, you may do more harm than good. This does not mean trying to be a friend instead of a parent. It does mean you need to be able to empathize with your teenager to help him make the best decisions possible, even if they are hard ones to make.

I hope you will find this book to be a useful resource. Think of it as a starting point, and realize that you may need to do additional reading or seek out professional help in order to develop a comprehensive plan to help your teenager.

Best wishes on your success—both you and your teenager deserve to live a life that is not dominated by stress.

STRESS-
PROOF
YOUR TEEN

1
Peer pressure

Stressful events are all around us. It doesn't matter wheth-er you're a child, teenager, or adult—we all face stress every day. However, for teenagers there are some sources of stress that tend to be particularly influential. One of them is peer pressure.

Peer pressure may be the biggest source of stress in a teenager's life. That shouldn't be surprising; most teenagers want to be accepted by their peers. They want to fit in and be liked, whether by wearing a particular brand or style of clothing, participating in certain sports or afterschool activities, or even doing things we'd rather they not—smoking, drinking, and taking drugs—all to avoid the possibility of being excluded or bullied by others.

Peer pressure can be good or bad. The phrase tends to

focus on the negative: teenagers being "coerced" into doing things because their friends are doing them. However, that's not always going to be the case. Friends can use peer pressure to help reinforce positive norms, such as staying out of trouble, being polite, and doing well in school. Obviously that depends on who the friends are.

There has been a great deal of research done on peer pressure. The authors of one study looked at the susceptibility of teens and the influence of peer pressure.[i] The findings indicated that teens who were more susceptible to peer pressure were more likely to engage in unhealthy behaviors. For example, they were more likely to have problems with alcohol and drugs compared to those adolescents not as susceptible. Results showed that future behaviors were impacted as well. Adolescents who were more susceptible to peer pressure were more likely to engage in problematic behaviors in the future. None of these findings should be too surprising. However, there were some other findings that you might not typically associate with this type of stress; for example, those who were more susceptible to peer pressure were more likely to develop symptoms of depression over time. Further, these kids were also more likely to lose their popularity. I would speculate that teenagers who easily give in to peer pressure lose the respect of their friends. Always giving in to what others want can be seen as degrading. Someone with no backbone can't be respected.

This highlights the need for teenagers to be individuals while being part of a collective group. Encouraging this individualism within the group is how you as a parent can help your teenager grow and manage stress. It is important to help your teen learn to navigate her own way and do what is right. At times this may mean going against something the peer group wants or believes in. It may also mean your teen has to make a break from the group and seek out new friends. Later sections in this book will provide you with suggestions to help your child deal with these issues.

One thing that people, especially teenagers, tend to be preoccupied with is weight and body image. Peer pressure has been shown to influence a teen's body weight: being thin and well-sculpted is ideal, while being overweight is frowned upon. On the one hand, if peers promote a healthy lifestyle in an appropriate manner (e.g., proper diet or exercise), then it can be beneficial. Unfortunately, body image and weight tend to be more important than how someone achieves it, which can result in an eating disorder such as anorexia or bulimia. These conditions pose serious physical and mental health problems.

A study published in 2008 found that friends do have an influence on body weight.[ii] The body weight of any given teenager was related to the body weight of that teen's friends. What is especially interesting is that this applied to teenage girls but not boys, as the female body tends to be more scrutinized than the male body. Another study found that peer pressure influenced eating behaviors.[iii] In this study the authors found that peer pressure to be thin led to eating disorders, and that peer pressure predicted changes in eating behaviors a year later. This shows that peer pressure can have long-lasting effects. The study also found that more pressure to be thin was placed on adolescent girls than boys. As I'll discuss in an upcoming chapter, approximately 90 percent of people with eating disorders are females. Women, especially teenage girls, are more prone to the pressures of achieving an ideal image.

For better or worse, peer pressure plays a significant role in the lives of our teens. It will be important to keep this in mind when trying to help your children deal with stress.

2
Low self-esteem

Self-esteem is one of the most important factors in dealing with stress. It can be either a source of stress (low self-esteem) or a protection against stress when it arises (high self-esteem). The March of Dimes defines self-esteem as "a combination of feeling loved and capable."[i] Others indicate that self-esteem refers to how a person thinks about herself. The National Association for Self-Esteem says it is "the experience of being capable of meeting life's challenges and being worthy of happiness."[ii] I look at this way: it is how you feel about yourself based on your life experiences.

A lifelong process

Self-esteem is developed over time, from childhood all

the way through adulthood. A person's self-esteem will fluctuate in response to life circumstances. For example, if your teenager fails an exam, gets dumped by a girlfriend or boyfriend, or does poorly in a sporting event, her self-esteem is going to take a temporary hit. On the flip side, if all those events have a positive outcome, the level of self-esteem will temporarily rise.

Research shows that self-esteem is generally the lowest during adolescence. This isn't surprising. With everything that is happening during this transitional period, it is easy for teenagers to doubt themselves, at least temporarily. Other major sources of stress also play a role here: peer pressure, concerns about school and a career, bullying, sexuality, conflicts among friends and family, and going through the wonderful experience of puberty.

Effects of low self-esteem

The impact self-esteem has on your teenager simply cannot be overstated. It influences everything—from developing and maintaining friendships to doing well in school to medical and emotional disorders. As a parent, one of the best things you can do is help build your child's self-esteem.

Low self-esteem not only influences stress—it can be affected by stress as well. Stress has a stronger influence on teenagers with low self-esteem, and because self-esteem influences the ability to solve problems, those with low self-esteem will have more difficultly finding healthy solutions to their problems. Unfortunately, this leads to more stress, which further lowers self-esteem.

Research has shown that self-esteem influences positive and negative behaviors. The authors of one study found that low self-esteem, along with stress and poor coping skills, influences eating attitudes that can result in eating disorders.[iii] Another result of low self-esteem is depression. Further, low self-esteem affects poor coping strategies.

There is concern that self-esteem during adolescence can have long-term effects. In other words, low self-esteem during the teenage years may translate into more problems during adulthood. However, the authors of one study looked at this question of whether teen self-esteem influences adulthood[iv] and found some encouraging results. These findings indicate that a teenager's level of self-esteem at age fifteen had either no relationship to, or a weak relationship to, substance dependence, mental health problems, life satisfaction, and relationship satisfaction. The environment the teenagers were raised in played a more significant role and had a more lasting effect.

3
School

Chances are, the older your teenager becomes, the more he'll worry about school and a career. There is pressure to do well in school. Then there's the pressure associated with going to college. What schools to apply to? How to pay for school? Is it worth going to college or is it better to go right out into the job force? These are not easy questions to answer, especially for adolescents. The biological changes and other stressors can make it difficult to concentrate, yet when it comes to an education and career, concentration is needed in order to make the right decisions.

Academic expectations

School is considered one of the most significant stressors for teenagers, partly due to factors discussed elsewhere in the book—peer pressure, bullying, and so on—and also because of pressure to do well in school. What kind of expectations do your children have about school? What are your expectations? It's bad enough for your teen to disappoint himself by not doing well. It can be even worse disappointing his parents. If too much pressure exists to do well, then there's an increased risk that your children won't do as well as they "should."

The authors of one study looked at stress in both high-achieving students and those in a general education program.[i] Not surprisingly, the authors found that students in the high-achievement group experienced more stress than those in the general education group. However, the higher level of stress did not hurt their academic achievements. This is actually the opposite of what other studies have shown—that more stress hurts grades.

School safety

There is another stressful aspect of school that should be considered: the school environment and overall safety. Every year we hear about cases in which teachers or students are violently injured or killed. And then there are instances in which kids are caught bringing weapons to school. It's also hard to forget the massacres that have happened, such as those at Columbine or Virginia Tech. These tragedies occur, and unfortunately, the media exploits them. In turn, that fosters further fears.

Every year the federal government publishes a report on school safety.[ii] This information will help put the reports you hear in the media into a better perspective. During the 2007–2008 school year there were approximately 55.7 million students enrolled in prekindergarten through twelfth grade. Less than half of one percent (0.5) of students ages twelve through eighteen indicated they had been a victim of physical violence. However, 32 percent of students indicated they had been bullied.

Further, there is some concern about the general atmosphere in schools. Ten percent of teachers in city schools indicated they had been threatened with injuries by students. This drops to six percent in suburban or rural areas. Approximately half of the teachers reporting the threats were physically attacked (five percent in city schools and three percent in rural schools).

In addition to that, students have to deal with gangs and drugs. According to the research, 20 percent of schools reported gang activities had taken place. For students in grades nine through twelve, 22 percent indicated they had been offered, sold, or given drugs while on school property. And 35 percent of students between the ages of twelve and eighteen reported seeing hate-related graffiti on school grounds.

We've all been through school and have dealt with problems and hassles. Even with that in mind, schools these days are different than those in the past. The point here is you should not assume you know what school is like for your teenager. Ask questions and learn as much as you can about your teen's experiences.

4
Bullying

No one likes a bully, especially teenagers who are the targets. And it seems that more and more news stories focus on school bullies. Just how big of a problem is bullying? Well, depending on the information you look at, it can be a small or large problem. For example, some research by the government indicates that approximately one-third of students between the ages of twelve and eighteen are bullied. The National Youth Violent Prevention Resource Center cites that 11 percent of students in grades six through ten are victims of bullies. Another 13 percent are bullies, and 6 percent are both bullies and victims.

Even worse is that bullying now happens over the Internet by sending harassing e-mails or instant messages. Creating demeaning or embarrassing Web sites about a person is another form of cyber-bullying. Online social isolation is another approach that happens when peers purposely ignore another's online presence.

You might think that your teenager will tell you if he is being bullied. Well, you might want to think again. Most teenagers do not tell their parents that they are being bullied. Research shows that teenagers are often embarrassed about being bullied and keep the problem to themselves. Others fear they will get in trouble because of their involvement. For example, someone who bullies and is a victim of bullying will not be likely to share his problems out of fear that he'll be punished for his own actions. Whatever the reason for not telling you, the result is the same: you're left in the dark.

Generally speaking, there are two types of bullying: physical and nonphysical. Physical bullying is self-explanatory—it's when the victim is hit, kicked, punched, spit on, and so on. Nonphysical involves name-calling, threats, spreading rumors, social isolation—the list goes on and on. Nonphysical bullying is more common than physical bullying, and it can leave permanent marks on your teenager.

Bullying can have serious consequences. It can cause depression and anxiety disorders to develop and can even lead some to attempt or commit suicide. In March 2010, nine teenagers were arrested for their alleged role in driving a girl to commit suicide. They were accused of bullying the girl to the point that she took her own life. This may be an extreme example of the consequences of bullying, but it underscores the type of pressure teenagers can feel because of it. Unfortunately, if you do an Internet search you will find plenty of instances in which victims of bullying attempted or successfully committed suicide.

Almost all kids get teased or picked on at some point. You can say that's a normal part of growing up. However, there is a difference between being occasionally picked on and being bullied. Ideally, neither should happen. As I'll discuss later on in the book, one of the best things you can do is have a quality relationship with your teen. This will help establish the trust needed for her to confide in you if bullying becomes a problem.

5
Divorce

Getting a divorce can be a significant source of stress for your teens. In fact, it can be so stressful on children that there are even support groups for adult children whose parents are getting divorced.

Some teenagers are glad their parents are divorcing. If the household has become so toxic because of parental fighting, even teens know life would get better if the parents split. Some teenagers act like it is cool to have divorced parents; many of their friends have divorced parents, so when their parents split up, it becomes one more thing they have in common. Either way, it doesn't mean there will not be any stress related to the divorce—just because a divorce will make the situation better doesn't mean the process is easier.

In addition to the family disruption caused by a divorce,

parents can actually make the situation worse. Unfortunately, there are many parents who don't hesitate to use their children against the other parent—pointing out all of the ex-spouse's bad qualities, making up lies, or exaggerating about problems. This can become even more problematic if the divorce is going to court and child custody issues have to be resolved. Some parents may feel they are no longer responsible for their teenager's well-being (sad, but true). A parent who decides to drop out of the teen's life can emotionally destroy that child.

Research has repeatedly shown that a divorce can cause teenagers to experience a variety of emotional, behavioral, and health problems. For example, teenagers from divorced families are more likely to use alcohol and drugs, experience depressive or anxiety disorders, get into trouble, have sex, and leave home early. What's worse is that the more serious the problems are or the longer they are present, the more likely they will continue into adulthood (or lead to even more problems in adulthood). It's not as if these problems are experienced by your teen one day and disappear the next day. After a divorce is finalized and everyone has forgotten about it, the long-term consequences may still linger. Therefore, it is very important not to assume that your teenager will be just fine.

6
Parental dating and remarriage

Another potential source of stress is parental dating and moms or dads getting married again. This applies only if you are getting or have obtained a divorce or your spouse has passed away. If you are married and are dating on the side, stop your behavior or at least shield your children from knowing about it.

If you date again, it can cause a great deal of stress for your teenager because he might think you are betraying the other spouse (or the spouse's memory). This will be especially true if you start going on a lot of dates with different people. Given what teenagers know (or think they know) about sex, they may label you as easy or slutty, or having no standards or morals. That will just create additional friction between the two of you. To help reduce this potential source of conflict, it's advised that you do not expose your teenager to your dates. If you start dating someone exclusively, then you may want to make introductions. It is strongly advised that you consult with a family therapist first to develop a strategy that will hopefully minimize any emotional trauma that could occur. If your significant other and teenager don't get along, then you should also seek counseling. That can be an ongoing source of stress for everyone involved.

If you decide to marry again, it can also cause additional stress for your teenager. This is an extension of the stress that can develop while you date. Once again, if your teenager and soon-to-be spouse don't get along, your teenager will feel even more stressed and might develop a sense of hopelessness about the situation. Your teenager may feel she is losing you since you will be devoting more of your life toward another person. A new family dynamic may emerge that your teenager doesn't like. It may include new rules and expectations. If your new spouse also has children, then there will be an expectation for all of them to get along. Problems with "playing favorites" or having different standards for everyone may develop.

Obviously, you have a right to move on with your life. However, it is important to remember that moving on with your life means your teenager also has to move on with your life. Whether we like it or not, our decisions can have a negative impact on our children's emotional well-being.

7
Family conflict

You can pick your friends but not your family. So the saying goes when people complain about their families. I'm willing to bet that your family has conflict in it. Maybe it's not too bad or unusual. You may have regular disagreements with your teens as they try to become more independent. Maybe there are issues with your spouse, creating temporary tension and arguments—you know, the daily hassles of life. Hopefully your house isn't characterized by perpetual arguments or violence. If that's the case, then your children are under a great deal of stress, whether you realize it or not.

Unlike many of the other chapters, I'm not going to reference any studies or provide basic statistics here. Whereas it may be useful to learn more about other sources address-ing family stress, you know what goes on in your home.

If you are always arguing with your kids, then they are going to be less likely to confide in you when they have a problem. Research does show that teenagers will "manage" what information you know about. The more they believe you will disapprove of their behavior, the less likely they'll talk. After all, why get into another argument because, ac-cording to your teen, "you just don't understand"? I'm pretty sure that comment about "not understanding" is something we've all told our parents.

Conflict at home can be difficult. Home is supposed to be the safe place to go. However, when there is constant ar-guing or if the threat of violence exists, home can be more stressful than dealing with others at school. If your teenager doesn't want to come home, where is he going to go? Or what will he be doing? It's pretty stressful for a teenager to have to deal with this. And this stress impacts other areas of his life. It's been shown that a stressful home environment hurts a teenager's grades, ability to concentrate, self-esteem, ability to cope in a healthy manner, relationships with other people—and the list goes on. The more severe the domestic conflict, the more problems your teenager will likely expe-rience in other areas of his life. And that can cause more arguments between you and your teen, which adds to stress at home, which causes more problems . . .

8
Friends and dating

Setting aside peer pressure for a minute, friends can be stressful. As we all age, even during our adolescent years, our interests can start changing. Priorities change. Friends change. If your teenager is drifting away from her friends, that will create some stress (even if the change is ultimately for the best).

Then there are always disagreements and arguments. And gossip. Even among friends, gossip happens. Feelings can get hurt. From your teenager's point of view, life can't get any worse!

At the same time, having no friends, or not enough friends, can be stressful, leading to depression and social isolation. The same goes for dating—if your teen is not at least occasionally dating, then his self-esteem may take a hit.

Of course, there are always the instances when your teenager falls in love and knows "this is the one." Then the following week things go right down the toilet, and they have to deal with the heartache that will "never end." It also doesn't help that the body is going through hormonal changes because of puberty. We know that life will get better, but unfortunately, our children think we don't understand because "this is different!"

The dark side to dating

There is a dark side associated with teenage dating. That's teen dating violence. Adults aren't the only ones who can be involved in abusive relationships. Some estimate that about 33 percent of teens experience violence in their relationships. According to a fact sheet published by the American Bar Association, teens may be at a higher risk of dating violence than adults. The ABA cites a study out of California that found half of reported date rapes occur among teenagers.[i] If your teenager is dating, please do not assume everything is fine, especially if you have a daughter. Pay attention to signs and behavior changes that may indicate she is in an abusive relationship.

9
Puberty

Puberty is the process that occurs when the body becomes sexually mature. It begins around age twelve for girls and age thirteen for boys and can last from two to four years. As I'm sure you know, puberty causes kids to go through plenty of changes. Body features develop, and the ability to reproduce begins. Boys experience voice changes and develop body odor, acne, body hair, pubic hair, and muscle. Girls will also develop pubic hair, body odor, and acne, and their body shapes begin to change. Breasts will also develop at this time, which can be a source of embarrassment for many teenage girls.

Influences of puberty and early onset

Evidence does indicate that puberty influences stress and coping skills. In one study it was discovered that the early onset of puberty caused problems for girls.[i] In cases where puberty started early, girls experienced more psychological problems. Since the body and mind grow together but not at precisely the same rates, it may be that girls are not psychologically ready to deal with puberty if it starts early.

Puberty can influence your teenager's level of anxiety and depression. One recent study found that puberty was a significant predictor of depression in both boys and girls.[ii] Once again, those teenagers who started puberty early were more likely to be depressed than those who were normal or late starters. Furthermore, another study found that the timing of puberty influenced cigarette and alcohol use:[iii] teenagers who started puberty early were twice as likely to try cigarettes and more than three times as likely to try alcohol.

And if this weren't problematic enough for teenagers, here's another wrinkle. Kids who experience chronic stress can start experiencing puberty early which, in turn, can cause more stress.

It is important to remember that puberty is a trying time for teenagers. Between the physical, social, and psychological pressures that occur, the body can be overwhelmed. In particular, a teenager's brain can become overwhelmed. This can cause anxiety, depression, and the inability to cope with life's stressors. Be patient and talk with your teen about the psychological and physical effects of puberty, reassuring them that the changes they are going through are normal. Doing so will help ease their concerns during this transitional period and encourage them to open up about problems they might be having.

10
Sex and sexuality

Another source of stress for teenagers is sex and their sexuality. As you know, puberty creates plenty of changes in the body. This includes developing sexual urges and exploring sexuality. It's not uncommon for teenagers to initially feel uncomfortable with the changes they are experiencing.

Many teens become sexually active, despite hopes from parents to hold off. Worse, many parents are under the impression that their own teenagers are refraining from such behaviors while other teens are "irresponsible." However, the Centers for Disease Control and Prevention (CDC) found in 2007 that 48 percent of high school students had already had sex, with 35 percent currently active. You may find it even more surprising that 15 percent had already been with at least four different partners. Unfortunately, 39 percent of high school students do not use a condom during sex. If they develop a sexually transmitted disease or get pregnant, their stress levels will increase exponentially.

At this point, some teenagers will also question their sexuality. Are they straight? Gay? Indifferent? Even more stressful is how their friends and family might react if they aren't straight. Teenagers who are gay, lesbian, bisexual, or transgendered (LGBT) experience more stress and are at an increased risk for self-harm and suicide. They are also more likely to be bullied and discriminated against, as the authors of one study found.[i] Their research results showed that teenage males in the LGBT category experienced more discrimination than LGBT girls. Both LGBT males and females were more likely to experience depression, suicidal thoughts, and engage in self-harm. A 2010 study found similar results.[ii] Compared to straight teenagers, those who were gay, lesbian, bisexual, or unsure of their sexual orientation were more than twice as likely to feel sad or hopeless. They were almost three times more likely to consider suicide and 3.5 times more likely to attempt suicide.

Obviously, sexuality is a significant stressor for teenagers. Think about your own experiences when you were a teenager. Were you unsure of your sexuality? Did you discover that you were gay or lesbian and didn't feel safe to share this with your friends and family? Did others accuse you of being gay or lesbian? Maybe you knew someone who was the target of such gossip. What kind of impact did that sort of gossip and bullying have? If your teenager is questioning his or her sexuality, or is being confronted by gossip and rumors, you can bet there is a tremendous amount of stress associated with it. Encourage your teen to talk with you about this stress they may be experiencing.

11
Anxiety

One of the most common reactions to stress is anxiety. Stress can cause your teenager to become worried, fearful, agitated, or uneasy. Physical reactions to anxiety include bodily tension, fatigue, headaches, nausea, chest pain, difficulty breathing, shortness of breath, twitching, insomnia, and more.

Anxiety can be a temporary or chronic state. Temporary anxiety is an understandable response to stressful events. Chronic anxiety is a serious problem and even takes a significant toll on the body, in which it is not working in a normal fashion. The continuing anxiety may be triggered by chronic stress, or an anxiety disorder may have developed which keeps the body in an anxious state even when no stressors are present.

Types of anxiety

There are several types of anxiety disorders. Generalized anxiety disorder (GAD) is a common one your teenager can suffer from. Individuals with this disorder are chronically anxious. According to the National Institute of Mental Health Web site, generalized anxiety disorder "is an anxiety disorder characterized by chronic anxiety, exaggerated worry, and tension, even when there is little or nothing to provoke it." A diagnosis of GAD is given when a person worries excessively about everyday problems for at least six months.

Another type of anxiety disorder is obsessive-compulsive disorder (OCD). The National Institute of Mental Health says that OCD "is characterized by recurrent, unwanted thoughts (obsessions) and/or repetitive behaviors (compulsions)." Examples of OCD include repetitive hand washing, counting, checking, and constantly cleaning. Obsessive thoughts can focus on almost anything, such as being worried about coming into contact with germs, being afraid of social embarrassment, being afraid of hurting someone, and so on. These obsessions cause people with OCD to engage in compulsive behaviors. Washing one's hands until they are raw is an example. Repeatedly checking to make sure a door is locked before leaving is another. It's common for people to make sure their door is locked when leaving; however, those with OCD will repeatedly check the door in a very short period of time.

Another anxiety disorder is panic disorder. This occurs when someone has unpredictable panic attacks. Nothing in the immediate area acts as a trigger for the panic. Think of it as a faulty "panic" switch that is randomly turned on. When it comes on, a person can suddenly have difficulty breathing, become dizzy, have a tight chest, break out into a sweat, faint, and so on.

Social phobia, or social anxiety disorder, is another type of anxiety disorder. The National Institute of Mental Health says that social phobia is characterized by "overwhelming anxiety and excessive self-consciousness in everyday social situations." Those with a social phobia are extremely worried that others are watching and judging them. They worry about doing anything that may be seen as embarrassing. They scrutinize everything they wear, say, or do in order to avoid humiliating themselves. Social phobia should not be confused with having a specific phobia, such as a fear of flying or spiders. Both are anxiety disorders; however, social phobia causes more anxiety for a sufferer.

Post-traumatic stress disorder can occur after experiencing a traumatic event. This could be a car accident, a natural disaster, a violent encounter, and so forth. The National Institute of Mental Health says that PTSD can occur "after exposure to a terrifying event or ordeal in which grave physical harm occurred or was threatened." Symptoms involve having flashbacks of the event while awake or dreaming. Those suffering from PTSD may avoid people, places, or situations that remind them of the event. Another symptom is hyperarousal, which refers to being easily startled or always "on alert."

What you can do

Experiencing anxiety or suffering from an anxiety disorder can cause a lot of problems for your teenager. Because of all the psychological, social, and physical changes your teenager experiences, it is easy to understand why many develop an anxiety disorder. As a parent, keep an eye on your teenager's behavior. If he is constantly acting fearful or "edgy," then try to find out what is going on. If the appearance of anxiety or fear is chronic, you should talk with both a counselor and a doctor. The sooner you can diffuse the problem, the better it will be for your teenager.

12
Extreme social phobia

As I mentioned in Chapter 11, social phobias are social anxiety disorders. As with any disorder, a person can experience minimal to extreme symptoms. One extreme social phobia worth mentioning is agoraphobia.

Agoraphobia is an anxiety disorder in which a person fears being in certain places, especially public places. The fear arises because it may be embarrassing or difficult to get out of the place; fear may also occur when a person is worried about having a panic attack and not being able to get help for it. The anxiety created leads people to avoid places or situations. For some people, that means never leaving home because it is the only place where they can control their fears and anxiety. For others, it may mean avoiding crowds, theaters, malls, schools, and so on.

Agoraphobia can cripple a teenager's life, especially if it goes undiagnosed. You can have the brightest teenager on the planet, but if she suffers from agoraphobia and school triggers the panic, it is a serious problem. If your teenager is fearful of going out in public or of certain places, you should definitely find out why. As with other anxiety or depressive disorders, therapy and medications can be used to treat this condition.

13
Depression

Depression and anxiety can result from stress. These can be temporary states or longer lasting. For example, doing poorly on an exam or breaking up with a girlfriend can temporarily cause your teen to be depressed. However, feeling down about certain events tends to be normal and will pass. If it doesn't pass, or if your child is constantly down, there is more of a reason to be concerned.

Major depressive episodes and disorders

A few depression-related definitions are needed to make sure we're on the same page. First, there is the major depressive episode (MDE). This is characterized by being depressed, or having a loss of interest in daily activities, for at least two weeks. Someone who experiences major depressive episodes is said to have a major depressive disorder (MDD). There are two types of MDD: single-episode and multiple-episode. If a person experiences one major depressive episode, comes out of it, and doesn't experience another, it is considered single-episode. However, if a person has a major depressive episode, gets better, has another sometime down the road, gets better, has another episode, and so forth, that is obviously considered multiple-episode MDD.

Symptoms

Depression affects the whole body—it is not simply a "psychological problem." Further, there are multiple causes of depression. Once again, it's not a psych problem people develop because they can't handle life. There are biological and genetic factors involved with depression. If you have been diagnosed with depression, then your children are at an increased risk of having it as well. How can you tell if they are suffering from depression?

First, your teen will have a depressed mood for most or all of the day. Irritability can also be an accompanying symptom of depression in children and adolescents. Second, your teen will have lost interest in daily activities for most of the day. Third, your teen may lose or gain a significant amount of weight that cannot be explained by diet—depression causes some people to lose their appetites and others to have increased appetites, particularly for "comfort" foods.

Sleep disruptions can also occur in those suffering from MDD. There will be a change in sleep patterns—too much sleep or having trouble sleeping. Those with MDD also feel tired or fatigued most of the time. They simply lack the energy to get through the day effectively.

Another symptom of depression is referred to as "psychomotor agitation or retardation." Those are simply big words that refer to unintentional body motions or physical gestures. Chronically tapping the foot or twirling hair or pacing around are examples of agitation. Psychomotor retardation is the opposite; it refers to physical activity being slowed down. You can think of it as acting lethargically: it takes a person longer to eat or talk or walk and so on. You're more likely to witness this in people with MDD. Either way, pay attention to how your teenager is acting and compare it to his or her normal actions.

Yet another symptom of depression is feeling worthless or excessively guilty on a daily basis. Because of these feelings, it should not be surprising that people with MDD may also have recurring thoughts of death. This includes thinking about suicide, thinking about and developing a plan for suicide, and attempting suicide.

The Substance Abuse and Mental Health Services Administration, part of the U.S. Department of Health and Human Services, conducts an annual survey on children as young as twelve on drug use and mental health issues. The survey found that in 2008, approximately 2 million kids between twelve and seventeen had a major depressive episode.

For 1.5 million of them, the episode was so severe that it affected school, family, and social lives.

Males versus females

Depression is more common in female adolescents than males. In fact, according to the Substance Abuse and Mental Health Services Administration survey, girls are nearly three times more likely to experience MDE (with and without severe impairment): slightly more than 12 percent of teenage girls experienced MDE compared to a little more than four percent of boys. Teenagers who are sixteen years old are most likely to experience a major depressive episode. The data show that 11.6 percent of sixteen-year-olds reported an MDE, with seventeen-year-olds coming in second at 10.6 percent. The percentages consistently dropped for those ages fifteen and younger.

14
Eating disorders

One very nasty reaction to stress is developing an eating disorder. There are three main types of eating disorders found in teens: anorexia nervosa, bulimia nervosa, and binge eating. Unfortunately, I am very familiar with eating disorders, as a member of my family ended up being hospitalized because of bulimia.

The National Eating Disorders Association (NEDA) says that anorexia nervosa (or just anorexia) is characterized by self-starvation and excessive weight loss. People who suffer from anorexia will purposely not eat enough during the day in order to lose a lot of weight. To them, there is no such thing as being "thin enough."

Bulimia nervosa, or simply bulimia, occurs when someone eats but then purposely finds a way to get rid of the food.

Vomiting, also known as purging, is what most people think of when hearing about bulimia. Many bulimics will eat and then go to the bathroom and make themselves throw up the food. It is also common for bulimics to abuse laxatives or diuretics (water pills) to help lose weight. Most bulimics, however, will binge on food and then purge it.

Binge eating occurs when someone frequently eats excessive amounts of food in a short period of time. Unlike with bulimia, no purging action is taken after binge eating.

Teenagers are especially prone to eating disorders. Specifically, female teenagers are at risk, and the majority of people of any age with an eating disorder are female. However, approximately 10 to 15 percent of those with an eating disorder are male. Please don't think that you have nothing to worry about regarding this issue if your teenager is a male. It could happen to your son.

The National Association of Anorexia Nervosa and Associated Eating Disorders (ANAD) reports that 43 percent of people with an eating disorder develop it by age fifteen. Another 43 percent develop the disorder between the ages of sixteen and twenty. Only 14 percent of cases develop an eating disorder after the age of twenty. Based on age alone, your teenager is in a high-risk group for developing an eating disorder. The Association also reports that an estimated 6 percent of those with serious cases die.

Having said that, most teenagers do not develop a clinical eating disorder. The National Eating Disorders Information Center, located in Canada, estimates that between 0.3

and 1.0 percent of adolescent and young women suffer from anorexia or bulimia. Those are conservative estimates and do not take into account teenagers who have unhealthy eating habits that are not considered full-blown eating disorders.

Anorexia and bulimia can cause serious physical problems, including malnutrition and dehydration. Damage can also be done to the heart, liver, and kidneys. In anorexics, bone density can drop, muscle loss occurs, and overall weakness and fatigue become evident. None of this should be surprising since the body is not getting enough nutrition to work properly.

Those who suffer from bulimia will damage their throats, gums, and teeth. The stomach acid is the reason for this—when the teen purges, the acid eats away the lining and tooth enamel. The family member I mentioned earlier now has to be checked periodically for cancer in her esophagus—she did that much damage to herself during her years of eating and purging. There's also been a significant amount of damage to her teeth, which has resulted in numerous root canals. If a bulimic is abusing laxatives, then bowel movements can become problematic, and constipation will occur. This also causes an electrolyte imbalance, which can damage the heart.

Teenagers who suffer from anorexia or bulimia are very preoccupied with body image. Because they believe they are "too fat," they have a strong desire to lose weight . . . then more weight . . . and more weight. In addition to reducing food intake, becoming obsessed with exercise is another way for anorexics and bulimics to lose weight and improve (or at least believe they are improving) their body image.

It is extremely important to question your teenager if you notice rapid weight loss. Be wary of vague answers such as, "I'm just not hungry lately," or "Everything's fine. I don't know what's going on." If you notice your teenager going to the bathroom after every meal, it may not hurt to silently follow and listen for vomiting noises. Your teen may not appreciate it, and some may think you're being sneaky. But being temporarily looked down upon if it will help you get the proper help for your teen is worth it.

15
Alcohol use

Depression in teens strongly correlates to drug and alcohol use. The 2009 study by the Substance Abuse and Mental Health Services Administration (SAMHSA) found that depression was related to drug, alcohol, and cigarette use among youth between the ages of twelve and seventeen. Those with a major depressive episode were twice as likely to admit regularly drinking large amounts of alcohol in the past month. Although that percentage was low—3.4 percent versus 1.8 percent—experiencing a major depressive episode was a risk factor for smoking and drinking.[i]

Underage drinking

Overall, underage drinking is still a problem. Many teenagers think it's cool to drink often and get drunk. How many times have you either attended a party, or heard about one, where everyone was getting drunk? Although I never attended these parties growing up, every Monday there were discussions about who got wasted over the weekend. Teenagers, even young ones, have access to alcohol. Drinking may help temporarily alleviate depression or anxiety, but problems grow worse if a teenager (or anyone) depends more and more on alcohol.

According to the SAMHSA study, almost 49 percent of people between eighteen and twenty admitted to currently using alcohol. Slightly more than 26 percent of sixteen- and seventeen-year-olds admitted to current alcohol use. This drops to 13 percent for teenagers who are fourteen or fifteen. Last of all, a little more than 3 percent of twelve- and thirteen-year-olds admitted to currently using alcohol.

Binge drinking

Binge drinking is also a problem, although not as much as regularly drinking alcohol. A third of those eighteen to twenty years old admitted to binge drinking. This drops to 17 percent for sixteen- and seventeen-year-olds, almost 7 percent for fourteen- and fifteen-year-olds, and 1.5 percent for those twelve to thirteen years old. Twelve- and thirteen-year-old kids binge drinking? That's a problem that calls for serious attention.

16
Drug use

In addition to alcohol, another way that teens try to cope with stress is to use drugs. If you think that there's no way your child uses or will ever use drugs, then you may want to reconsider. A recent (2009) report by the U.S. Department of Health and Human Services found that close to 10 percent of youth between the ages of twelve and seventeen were actively using illicit drugs. Slightly more than 3 percent of children ages twelve and thirteen indicated they used drugs. However, this number reaches 15 percent for those ages sixteen or seventeen. For those between eighteen and twenty, slightly more than 21 percent indicated current drug use.

Although the majority of teenagers do not actively use drugs, it does not mean you should dismiss the possibility that your teenager is drug-free. Statistics really don't matter if your teen is one of the few using drugs.

Common illegal drugs

A national study conducted every year, "Monitoring the Future," examines smoking, drug, and alcohol use among students in the eighth, tenth, and twelfth grades. Based on the latest results of this research, marijuana is the most commonly used drug (not including alcohol). According to data from 2009, almost 21 percent of high school seniors indicated they had used marijuana at some point in the last thirty days. This drops down to 16 percent for tenth-grade students and 6.5 percent for eighth-grade students. By comparison, only 1 to 2 percent of high school seniors indicated they had recently used drugs such as cocaine or ecstasy. Other drugs that we commonly think of, such as crystal meth, heroin, or crack, were used by less than 1 percent of high school seniors. Once again, the low probability of your teenager using one of these drugs becomes irrelevant if your teen actually uses one of them.

Prescription drug abuse

Chances are that when you think of drug abuse, the drugs I've mentioned above are what comes to mind. However, there is another type of drug abuse that is becoming more problematic: prescription drug abuse. Also referred to as nonmedical prescription use, access to prescription drugs may be only a room or two away. Are you or other family members on any medications that can alter a person's mental state? Painkillers like Oxycontin, Vicodin, or Dilaudid? Sedatives such as Valium, Xanax, or Ativan? Stimulants such as Ritalin or Adderall? If so, it is worth noting that many teenagers feel it is easier to obtain prescription drugs than street drugs. Teenagers have been known to steal medications from friends and family. The really brave ones will try to steal a prescription pad from a doctor's office, or alter the number of medications prescribed on a prescription pad.

One amusing example highlights the degree to which some teenagers will try to obtain prescription medications. An OB-GYN told me about an incident she experienced several years ago in which a teenage patient managed to steal one of her prescription pads. The girl was too scared to write a prescription for herself. So in a moment of "clarity," she decided to write it for her boyfriend. The pharmacist who took the script immediately knew it was not written by the doctor. How? Well, how many OB-GYNs do you know who have male patients? When the girl went to pick up the script, the police picked her up instead.

There is not as much research on the abuse of prescription drugs by teenagers as there is for illegal drugs. But based on the data that do exist, the overall problem has been increasing steadily for at least a decade. Once again, data from the Monitoring the Future study provides some insight into this problem. In 1991, approximately 1.4 percent of high school seniors admitted to using sedatives within the past thirty days. In 2009, that number went up to 2.5 percent. However, that is lower than 2002, when a high of 3.2 percent admitted to using sedatives.

Use of tranquilizers has shown a similar pattern. In 1991, 1.4 percent of high school seniors admitted to using tranquilizers within the past thirty days. This hit a high of 3.3 percent in 2003 and dropped to 2.7 percent in 2009. Narcotics, excluding heroin, hit a high of 4.3 percent in 2004 and were at 4.1 percent in 2009.

What you can do

Drug use by teenagers is a problem. It is not as prevalent as smoking, drinking, or being drunk; however, the consequences can be fatal, which is something no one wants. If you have prescription medications in the home, keep track of them. If you notice that the number of pills is fewer than it should be, then you should confront everyone in the home to determine whether anyone else is using them.

17
Smoking

One way to deal with stress is to smoke. Nicotine is an antidepressant and helps calm people's nerves. It's a stress reliever. How many times have you or someone else close to you needed to smoke a cigarette to calm down?

There's no need to spend a great deal of time on why smoking isn't a good idea. It's addicting. People who smoke have more medical problems than those who don't smoke. Cigarettes contain chemicals that are known to cause cancer. And the list goes on. If you're interested in learning more about smoking, plenty of resources are listed in this book.

If your teenager is under the age of eighteen, he should not have access to cigarettes. Well, that's the law, anyway. In reality, that doesn't mean much, as minors can easily obtain cigarettes, either themselves or through another person.

However, research shows that smoking has been declining among teenagers for about a decade. In 2008, only 11.2 percent of twelfth-grade students indicated they smoked on a daily basis. Only 6.3 percent of tenth-grade students smoke daily, and slightly less than three percent of eighth-grade students smoke every day. However, more students in all grades admit to having smoked at least once during the past thirty days.

Research also shows that teenagers who have experienced a major depressive episode are twice as likely to smoke when compared to those without an MDE. The SAMHSA research cited in the prior chapter also looked at smoking data and confirmed this statistic. According to those findings, slightly less than 4 percent of teens between ages twelve and seventeen who had a major depressive episode in the past year admitted to smoking on a daily basis, while almost 2 percent of teens without an MDE in the past year admitted to smoking daily.

Smoking has become less popular over the years. However, that does not stop underage teenagers from trying cigarettes or using them on a regular basis, especially if they are stressed. Luckily, as a parent, you can easily discover whether your teenager smokes—the smell on them or their clothing will give it away.

18
Risky sexual behaviors

Sex can be a great stress reliever. After all, it's physical exercise that takes your mind off other problems and can be a lot of fun in the process. Not to mention the chemical reactions that happen in the body that help with people's moods. You can even "learn" a lot about great sex just by reading the various magazines found at the checkout lines in grocery stores!

The teenage years are when most kids start thinking and experimenting with sex. The Centers for Disease Control and Prevention publishes an annual report on sexual behavior among the nation's youth. The CDC found that in 2009, 46 percent of high school students admitted to having sex at least once in their lives. This ranged from a low of about a third of ninth graders to almost two-thirds of high school seniors. Slightly more than a third of all students indicated they were currently sexually active. Only 21 percent of those in the ninth grade indicated this, while half of seniors acknowledged they are sexually active. One surprising finding is that females are more likely to be sexually active than males. If you believe the traditional stereotypes, then it should be the other way around.

Unfortunately, many teenagers don't practice safe sex. Overall, 61 percent of those who are sexually active use a condom during sex. That means nearly 40 percent of sexually active teenagers are not practicing safe sex. You would think as teenagers grew older that they would be more likely to practice safe sex. Apparently not. Students in the tenth grade were most likely to use condoms, with almost 68 percent indicating this. Only 55 percent of seniors admitted to using condoms during sex. Considering that close to 90 percent of high school students are taught about HIV and AIDS, not to mention the more common sexually transmitted diseases and infections they are taught about, the number of students who use condoms is pretty dismal.

Evidence indicates that there is a relationship between depression and sexual behavior. Teenagers who engage in risky sexual acts (e.g., not practicing safe sex, having multiple partners, using drugs or alcohol right before sex) end up being more depressed than those who don't engage in such acts. Instead of using sex as a way to temporarily reduce depression, risky sexual behaviors increase the likelihood of depression.

19
Nonlethal self-injury

There are two types of self-injury: nonlethal—physically hurting oneself—and lethal, or suicide. The authors of one professional study say that non-suicidal self-injury "is most commonly described as deliberate, direct destruction or alteration of body tissue without conscious suicidal intent."[i] In other words, it's when someone tries to hurt himself without trying to kill himself. It is very important to know, however, that self-injury is a risk factor for suicide. In other words, the risk of suicide increases if your teen engages in a form of nonlethal self-injury.

What kinds of self-injuries are there?

Teens can use a number of different strategies to injure

themselves. One of the most common is cutting. This is pretty self-explanatory: a teen takes a sharp object and repeatedly cuts her skin. Other forms of self-injury include picking, burning, pulling hair, hitting body parts, consuming toxic substances, and preventing wounds from healing.

I would know if my teen is injuring herself . . . right? You may think it's easy to know whether your teenager is inflicting injuries to herself. Well, think again. Most of your body is covered by clothing. Depending on the style of clothing your teenager wears and where she inflicts herself, it can be easy to cover up wounds.

How many teens practice self-inflicting behavior?

It is hard to tell how prevalent non-suicidal self-injury is. One recent study indicates that the estimates vary greatly, ranging from 10.5 percent all the way up to 46.5 percent.[ii] In my own study, I found that almost 44 percent of adolescents had reported various forms of self-injury during the past year, with scratching and cutting as the two most common forms. Some research indicates that the typical onset of self-injury behavior happens between ages fourteen and twenty-four.[iii] That's a pretty broad range. However, it appears that this problem peaks among kids ages twelve to fourteen and then eighteen to nineteen.[iii]

Why is my teen doing this?

So why is it that people engage in self-harm? It appears that teens who engage in this type of behavior have difficulty regulating their emotions and so relieve them in this manner. These emotions include guilt, loneliness, anxiety, depression, and self-hatred. Self-injury is also used to help release anger and emotional pain.[i] Physically harming oneself can, unfortunately, help a person deal with their emotions, just as eating or exercising can.

Self-injury also helps people feel in control. The authors of one study found that the three most common reasons for self-harm included getting a reaction from someone, gaining control over a situation, and helping them to stop feeling bad.[i] Also, this type of behavior can be a distraction from the problem. The pain distracts the mind, at least temporarily.

What can I do?

If you notice your teenager has injuries, find out what happened. Also, if he is wearing clothing that is inappropriate for the weather conditions, see what's going on. Wearing long pants and a long-sleeve shirt on hot and humid summer days doesn't seem right. Don't chalk it up to your teenager being eccentric.

20
Suicide

Some people, and many teens, view suicide as the only way to get rid of their stress. According to the Centers for Disease Control and Prevention (CDC), during 2006, suicide was the eleventh leading cause of death in the U.S. for people at least ten years old. However, it is the *third* leading cause of death for teenagers between the ages of fifteen and nineteen. I cannot understate the significance of this finding.

Males versus females

Research shows that female high school students are more likely than male students to think about and attempt suicide. The CDC indicates that in 2007, almost 19 percent of female students in grades nine through twelve—about one out of five—had seriously considered suicide within the past year, while just over 10 percent of males had given it serious consideration. Slightly more than nine percent of females made an attempt, while less than five percent of males made an attempt. And approximately 2.4 percent of females and 1.5 percent of males made an attempt that resulted in the need for medical attention. Other data indicates that in 2006, there were close to 2,000 suicides committed by people between the ages of twelve and nineteen.

Methods

There are several ways to commit suicide. These include using firearms, overdosing, jumping, hanging, slitting wrists, and driving into objects, among other things. The most common method of suicide is using a firearm. Of all suicides among youth, 47 percent involve firearms.

Warning signs

There are several warning signs associated with suicide that can help you determine whether your teen is at risk. The American Association of Suicidology uses the following phrase to know the warning signs: "IS PATH WARM?" This stands for:

I - Ideation

S - Substance abuse

P - Purposelessness

A - Anxiety

T - Trapped

H - Hopelessness

W - Withdrawal

A - Anger

R - Recklessness

M - Mood changes

If your teenager starts giving her personal belongings away, don't assume she's just being generous. Giving away personal belongings, especially the ones she's most attached to, is a big warning sign. If your teenager starts engaging in risky or reckless behavior that can cause death, get help. Any talk about "not caring about life" or "believing the world will be better without me" is another major warning sign. Honestly, it's better to overreact and intervene than to not do enough and have your teenager take her life.

21
Behavioral changes

Considering that our behavior is a partial reflection of our mood, one of the best ways to determine whether your teen is struggling or is stressed out about something is to watch for any changes in behavior.

Signs of change

The American Psychological Association publishes an information sheet that deals with signs of stress in children and teenagers, attributing behavioral changes to stress. The APA states that if your child starts significantly avoiding you or becomes hostile to you or others in the family, it can be a sign of significant stress. If your teen is normally talkative and responsive and that begins to change, find out why. To some degree, this gradual avoidance can be expected as teenagers develop more independence. It may be more difficult to spot these gradual changes, but at some point, you should realize things have changed, and then it is important to see what's going on. Abrupt changes should definitely be acted upon.

The Association also writes that if your teenager abandons one group of friends for another, that can indicate a potential problem. On one hand, if your teenager stops hanging out with troublemakers and becomes friends with more responsible peers, that should be a good thing. But if the opposite happens, that's not such a good thing. Once again, find out why the change.

Another sign that something may be going on is if your teenager's energy level changes. Is she more lethargic and tired? More energetic and antsy? The former can be a sign of depression or unhealthy behavior, such as eating a lot of junk food. The latter can indicate anxiety. Pay particular attention to eating behaviors. If your teen starts adhering to an overly strict diet, doesn't want to eat, skips meals, or binges, those are signs of an eating disorder. If your son or daughter eats and then heads straight for the bathroom, that can be a sign of purging.

As I've mentioned repeatedly, the key is to know what is "normal" for your teenager so you can know when changes are taking place. If you suspect behavioral changes are occurring, talk to your teenager. It is also worth talking to school officials and your pediatrician, or a therapist, to see what you should do.

22
Mood changes

One of the biggest signs that your teen is having trouble with stress is mood changes. If your teenager makes abrupt changes in his mood, try to find out why. If she is normally happy and turns gloomy, ask what is going on. More important, if that mood change continues for a while or gets worse, definitely get involved.

Obviously there are going to be short-term changes in mood. Getting a job, failing an exam, being beat by another sports team, and so on will make your teen's mood fluctuate. But those fluctuations should be temporary.

Is your teen's normal mood changing?

You need to know what your teen's mood is normally

like. Is she normally happy, mellow, somewhat anxious, or reserved? Is she optimistic or pessimistic? Whatever your teen's regular mood is should be your starting point. Then you need to see whether it is changing. How is it changing? Is he becoming more optimistic? More anxious? Happier or sadder? If these changes appear to be lasting, ask why there's been a change.

If you suspect mood changes, ask other people for their observations. If others don't notice the same thing, then maybe you have to see whether there's a problem with your relationship with your teen. The altered mood may just be around you or others in the home. It's important to know that to better understand any sources of stress.

Signs of change

If your teenager is experiencing depression, you may notice he is more irritable or pessimistic. He will appear sad and maybe even anxious. Other feelings associated with depression include worthlessness, guilt, helplessness, and confusion, all of which play into one's mood. Unfortunately, the feelings and moods associated with anxiety—irritability, restlessness, confusion, and pessimism—are pretty close to those of depression, so it's important to learn the differences to be able to notice them in your teen.

What you can do

Should you notice mood changes in your teenager, take her to see the pediatrician. There are ways the doctor can screen for anxiety and depressive disorders. A child psychologist or psychiatrist can also determine whether depression or anxiety has become an issue.

23
Sleep patterns

You probably know from experience that there's a direct relationship between stress and sleep. Stress can cause people to not sleep enough or sleep too much. Occasionally having difficulty sleeping is normal. If your child has something stressful coming up, such as a big test, there will probably be a few restless nights. On a normal basis, though, teenagers should get approximately nine hours of sleep every night.

Depression can cause adolescents to sleep too little or too much. In one article the authors indicate that more teens tend to sleep too much from depression after they've hit puberty.[i] However, insomnia is still the dominant sleep problem because of depression. This can result in your teen sleeping longer in the mornings because of difficulty falling asleep, or your teen may be tired throughout the day or unable to concentrate. Worse yet, the lack of sleep can make depression even worse, which creates a nasty cycle (depression = lack of sleep = deeper depression).

Stress in general hurts not only the quantity of sleep but also the quality of sleep a person receives. The more stressed or worried someone is, the worse that person sleeps. The authors of some studies have even found that the degree to which a person worries about problems at bedtime influences the degree of quality sleep.

Pay attention to your teen's sleeping patterns. If she starts staying up late, or waking earlier than normal, see why. If she is having trouble sleeping, there are plenty of relaxation techniques and sleep aids that can be tried. When stress is the cause of insomnia, helping to reduce the stress should help improve sleep. Try to get to the heart of the matter to help your child relieve the underlying stress.

When your teen gets enough sleep and is still chronically tired, depression may be to blame. To best assess this, you and your child should talk with a doctor. Your teenager may not be depressed but may have a sleep disorder instead. A sleep study can be performed to see how well your teen is sleeping and help design a treatment strategy if problems do exist.

24
Eating patterns

Because teenagers are at risk for eating disorders, you should keep an eye on their eating behaviors. Many people with eating disorders do an excellent job hiding the disorder. This is especially true for those suffering from bulimia, because bulimics will eat and then go and purge (vomit) the food just eaten.

Stress is known to make people lose their appetite. It also makes others reach for "comfort foods," known as emotional eating. If your teenager starts coming up with excuses not to eat and consistently does this, it can be a sign of anorexia and should be investigated. If your teenager starts eating large amounts of food in a short period of time, known as binge eating, it may be a sign of bulimia or binge eating. If you notice changes that are concerning, you should address them with your child. Depending on the answers you receive and your own intuition, you may want to talk to your child's doctor as well.

Other reasons for changing eating patterns

Your teen's eating habits may not indicate that an eating disorder has developed. Changes in eating patterns can also be a sign of depression. Doctors use the *Diagnostic and Statistical Manual of Mental Disorders* (currently the fourth edition) to guide diagnoses of mental disorders, including depression. The manual says that "significant" weight loss can be a sign of depression, assuming that the person is not on a diet and therefore expected to lose weight. According to the manual, if a person loses at least five percent of their body weight in a month, it may indicate depression.

The authors of a recent study highlight several difficulties that relate to eating behaviors and stress (particularly depression).[i] Weight changes are expected during puberty and adolescence, and the authors indicate that 50 percent of adult body weight is obtained during the adolescent years. The authors also state that physical activity tends to drop between the ages of thirteen and eighteen. Obviously this—not just quantity of food—can increase weight gain.

In one study the authors found that different forms of stress influenced emotional eating for boys and girls.[ii]

Tension and anxiety, worries, and perceived stress influenced emotional eating for girls, and for boys, confused mood affected emotional eating.

If you notice any abrupt or subtle changes in eating patterns, then make a mental note of it. If they persist, talk to your teen, and talk to your teen's doctor if stress is leading to poor eating habits.

25
Physical changes

As your teen grows up, her body will change. As I mentioned earlier in the puberty chapter, puberty causes the body to mature. It is expected that your teen will gain some weight and that physical changes will occur. This can make it difficult to determine whether stress is having a negative impact on the body.

If you feel your teenager is gaining too much weight, ask about his eating habits. Ask your pediatrician whether this is normal. The same goes if you feel your teen is losing too much weight, which, as discussed, could be a sign of an eating disorder or depression. Also take note of reasons your teen may be exercising excessively or stopping altogether, contributing to weight loss or gain. New injuries could be a sign of a problem as well: Is your teen getting into fights? In

an abusive relationship? Being abused by an authority figure? Inflicting the wounds herself?

Tracking physical changes in your teenager and de-
termining whether they are normal or related to stress is
difficult to do. Your teen's pediatrician is in the best position to see whether there are problems with your teenager's
growth. Unless there are rapid changes or noticeable injuries, you may not notice any problems. One piece of advice:
if you are concerned about mood or behavioral issues, pay
more attention to your teen's body. The combination of observations can help you determine whether there is a real
problem.

26
Observations from others

The point here is to pay attention to what other people are saying about your teenager. If someone points out a troubling observation, listen to it. Don't simply dismiss it because that person "doesn't understand" your son or daughter. In fact, others may be in a better position than you to notice problems. Why? More objectivity. This is your child we're talking about. And there are parents who don't want to admit a problem exists. It's easy to explain away behaviors or moods, and it's easy to deny a problem exists—especially if you believe that problem would reflect poorly on you as a mother or father. For parents who act like this, observations from others may be a saving grace and may "force" the parent to admit there's a problem.

Is the observation reliable?

With that in mind, here are some things to consider when listening to someone's observations. First, who is the person? A family member? Relative? A friend, teacher, coach, neighbor? The list goes on. What kind of relationship does this person have to your teen? Is it a personal or more formal relationship (e.g., student-teacher)? How familiar is this person with your teen's normal moods and behaviors? How credible does the person sound? Is there reason to believe this person has an agenda to cause your teenager problems? Perhaps most important, how do these observations differ from your own?

It's up to you to take all of these questions into consideration in order to help decide whether you should be concerned with someone else's observations. This is just one piece of the puzzle when trying to figure out whether your teenager is struggling with any issues that are causing stress.

27
Listening

As a parent I'm sure you know that one of the most important things you can do in your child's life is listen. It is important to listen to what your teenagers say . . . and do not say. Some of the most important things may be left unsaid.

There are a couple of reasons listening will help your teen manage stress. First, the act of sharing thoughts and feelings with someone who will listen tends to make people feel better, as it's no longer bottled up inside. (If it didn't, then a lot of therapists and counselors would be out of business.) Second, it shows you care and are there to help.

You also have to realize that your teenager may not want to talk with you about personal problems. Obviously it depends on your relationship and the nature of your teen-ager's problem. You can't force your child to talk to you.

I view listening as one part of being a good communi-cator. Two other parts include being able to hold open and engaging conversations, and temporarily suspending judg-ment or action when you hear something you don't like.

Teenagers engage in a great deal of information man-agement. That means disclosing certain activities, hiding others, mentioning only certain elements, or flat-out lying. If your teen thinks you are not willing to listen, or will listen to only certain things, there is more of an incentive not to be completely honest with you.

28
Holding open conversations

Another element of good communication is having open conversations. By this I mean you do not dominate the conversation. Don't continually interrupt your teenager. Obviously, there will be times you will want to interject and ask questions. However, don't interrupt every minute. You need to be patient. A conversation is a two-way street. If one person dominates it, it turns into a lecture. Patience and maintaining a degree of civility are necessary for meaningful conversations.

Definitely do not yell, scold, or lecture your teen. That is easier said than done. However, save it for later. There will be time to address the consequences of any behavior later on. The goal of having an open conversation is for your teen to share his troubles with you. It's not to start telling you about issues and then get verbally lambasted because of it. If you have a tendency to do this, once again there is an incentive for your teenager to not be completely honest with you. You don't want to shut down the conversation.

When you ask questions, don't be demeaning. A question such as "How could you be so stupid as to do that?" is not going to be very productive. Rephrasing the question to say "What made you decide to do that?" is a less inflammatory way to get an answer.

29
Suspending judgment

In order for your teenager to want your help, you have to be trustworthy. In some situations that may mean listening to what your teen has to say without getting upset (or too upset, anyway). You may not like what your teen has done, or is doing, but there is always time to deal with the problem. When your teen *wants* to talk to you, it is important to look at things from your child's perspective and withhold judgment.

There will be times when your teen's behavior creates more stress. Take bullying, for example. If your teen has bullied someone and it resulted in retaliation, that can induce stress. If your teen tells you something like this, put yourself in his position and try to understand why he engaged in the negative behavior in the first place. Don't rush to judgments no matter how stupid you think your teen's actions were.

From your point of view, suspending judgment is probably the hardest thing to do. However, if you're going to try to help your teen deal with stress, you need to understand what is going on and why your teen may be behaving in a particular way. Don't add to your teen's stress by immediately jumping to conclusions when you haven't considered his perspective. This doesn't mean you always withhold your judgment or that you refrain from taking necessary action. You are in a position of authority and need to do what's best for your child. But it's important to realize that doing what's best may involve you taking a detached approach for a little while.

30
Seeking counseling

Counseling can play a vital role in reducing your teen's stress. According to the U.S. Department of Health and Human Services, in 2008 there were 3.1 million youths between ages twelve and seventeen who received inpatient or outpatient treatment or counseling for behavioral and emotional problems. Another 11.8 percent of youths received services in an educational setting, while 2.9 percent received services in a general medical setting. Generally, girls are more likely than boys to receive mental health services.

Is one visit enough?

The overwhelming majority of youth needing services see someone multiple times. Twenty-nine percent saw someone between three and six times. Another 25 percent saw someone between seven and twenty-four times, while almost 12 percent had to see someone at least twenty-five times. If for whatever reason your child needs to be seen by a counselor for a while, don't worry about it. Most people—adults and children—need several visits to work out issues.

How do I find the right counselor?

There are several things you can do to find a good counselor. Call your teen's school and ask who they recommend. Call your pediatrician and ask for a recommendation. If both the school and the pediatrician recommend the same counselor, that's a positive sign the counselor is good. Also ask your friends who they recommend.

Under no circumstances should you ever believe a doctor who says all doctors are good. I find it amazing when I ask a doctor for a recommendation and am told, "You can see anyone at a certain practice." That's the politically correct answer since professionals don't want to bad-mouth each other. Push the issue if you're given a generic answer like that. Ask, "If you had to see a counselor, who would you go to?" If you still get a generic answer, you can either continue to push the issue or find someone else to ask. I'll admit that I have a bias against this sort of answer. Over the years I've dealt with a number of bad doctors that others have lumped into the "they're-all-good" category.

Another thing you can do is search the Internet. You can

also call your insurance company and ask for a listing of counselors in the area. You won't know who's good or bad, but at least you'll discover multiple options.

Don't assume that once you find a counselor you have to stick with that person. Use your judgment and listen to your teenager. Some counselors will not be a good match due to personality differences or treatment philosophy. If things don't work out with one counselor, look for another.

What if I can't afford counseling?

If you don't have insurance to cover counseling, ask your school for suggestions or call the local social services office to see what programs are available. If you go to church, talk to the pastor or priest to see whether they offer counseling or have on-site counselors available. A potential problem with this, however, is that your teen may not want to talk with someone who casts judgment on behaviors. The last thing your teen needs to hear is how they simply need to look for help from a higher power and refrain from sinful behavior.

What if my teen doesn't want to go?

Don't be surprised if your teenager is resistant to counseling. I've met plenty of teens who had to go through counseling, and not one of them was receptive to it at first. Many ultimately warmed up to the experience, but others fought tooth and nail until they quit or the counselor gave up. You and the counselor will have to discuss ways to get your teenager to open up if he's resistant. Just be warned—it probably won't be easy.

31
Seeking out medical help

Depending on the degree of stress and your teen's ability to cope with it, you may need to take her to a physician, either her pediatrician or a psychiatrist. Your teen may need to be placed on an antidepressant to help her deal with an emotional disorder.

Medical referrals

If your teen needs to see a child psychiatrist (a specialist who can provide psychological treatment and prescribe medications), then your teen's pediatrician will make a referral. As I mentioned in the prior chapter, ask who the best child psychiatrist is in the area. If you completely trust your pediatrician, then don't worry about who your son or daughter is referred to.

Don't be surprised if your pediatrician refers your teen to a specialist. More and more pediatricians and family doctors do not want to manage psychiatric medications. Using medications to manage anxiety or depressive disorders can be tricky. On top of that, there has been some research that indicates teenagers on antidepressants are at an increased risk for suicide. In fact, the Food and Drug Administration requires pharmaceutical companies to indicate with the prescription information an *increased* risk of having suicidal thoughts or attempting suicide. Having said that, some research indicates that teenagers on antidepressants are at a decreased risk for having suicidal thoughts or making a suicide attempt.

In my opinion (and remember, I'm not a medical doctor), based on the research I've read, I don't believe taking antidepressants increases the risk. However, because you have to consent to letting your teenager take antidepressants, you need to talk at length with the doctor about the potential side effects of the medication, and then both of you can determine whether your teenager should take it.

32
Seeking temporary hospitalization

If your teen is in serious or life-threatening danger due to stressful situations, hospitalization may be necessary. Grounds for having your teen taken to the hospital include suicide attempts and drug and alcohol addictions.

Suicide

If your teenager is serious about committing suicide or makes a suicide attempt, you will need to have him hospitalized for inpatient treatment. This is necessary to help keep your teenager safe and get him the help needed. Depending on what happened, your teen may need to spend a few days to more than a week at the hospital.

Drugs and alcohol

Temporary hospitalization may also be needed to treat drug or alcohol abuse. Withdrawing from drugs and alcohol is often a painful experience because the body has become used to functioning with those high volumes of addicting substances in the system, and has compensated for this abuse in an effort to function properly. Take away the drugs or alcohol, and the body has to readjust. This readjustment is the withdrawal process. Depending on how often your teen used drugs or alcohol, doctors may need to put him on medications to help control the withdrawal effects.

Outpatient treatment

It is very important to remember that the hospitalization will be temporary—the problems will not be solved once your teen leaves. She will need outpatient treatment to deal with the associated psychological issues. The treatment may be intense, and your teenager may have to attend individual or group sessions three to five days a week. Or a weekly or twice-a-week counseling session may be in order. The doctors involved in your teen's case will decide the best course of action once your teen is discharged.

Choosing—or not choosing—the hospital

If your teen is hospitalized, you may not have a choice in which hospital she will go to. Part of it depends on how many hospitals are in your area. If you live in a rural area where there is only one hospital, guess where your teen is headed. If you live in an area where there are multiple hospitals, then your insurance will probably dictate which one your teenager goes to. If you live near several hospitals and can decide where to go, then you may be able to choose. You should know that if your teenager has attempted suicide, is injured, and needs to be transported by ambulance, the EMTs are required to go to the nearest hospital. After she has been stabilized, options can be discussed about transferring her to another hospital, assuming you have the option.

33
Using alternative and natural stress relievers

One way to help your teenager deal with stress is to use alternative and natural stress relievers. These can include meditation and visualization, massage, and herbs and supplements.

Meditation and visualization

Meditation and visualization are two proven techniques to help lower stress levels. They can also help with mood disorders, such as anxiety and depression. These techniques are safe, and there is minimal cost associated with them.

Massage

Massage is another way to help reduce stress. As you

know, when we are stressed we tense up, which tightens our muscles. Massage will loosen the muscles and help induce relaxation. There are different types of massage, ranging from ones that simply help relax you to intense massages that really work the muscles to get all of the knots out. More intense massages may not feel good; however, they are not meant to feel good but rather to get the muscles functioning properly again.

Herbs and supplements

Using herbs and supplements is a popular way to help relieve stress and promote healthy sleep. There are a variety of these products on the market that include valerian root, melatonin, passionflower, magnesium, lavender, kava kava, St.-John's-wort, and plenty of others. If you are interested in these types of products, the best thing to do is go to your local health food store and ask what they recommend. If your child is taking a prescription medication, consult his doctor first to find out whether any of the herbs could interact with the prescriptions.

34
Changing diet

Making dietary changes can help your teenager's body handle stress. Stress causes the body to release a lot of chemicals so the body can rise up to challenges as they come. After the stress has subsided, the body returns to its normal state of functioning, as the body's "stress response" is meant to be short-term. Long-term or chronic stress means the body is constantly releasing chemicals and hormones. Without going into the science of it, the constant presence of these chemicals harms the body.

This is when a healthy diet can help. A healthy diet allows the body to maintain a healthy immune system and keeps energy levels up. Excessive stress hormones compromise the immune system, which increases the chances of your teenager becoming sick. The stronger your teen's immune system, the more stress he'll be able to handle before the body starts to break down.

Generally speaking, eating balanced meals and avoiding junk foods is the best way to go when it comes to regular diet. Have you counted how many aisles in a grocery store are dedicated to unhealthy foods? Soda, candy, chips, cookies, and other snacks should be avoided on a regular basis. Chances are you already know that, and hopefully your teenager knows as well. The problem is that a lot of the good-tasting food is the stuff that is typically bad for us. It also doesn't help that many restaurants serve food that tastes great but is pretty unhealthy for our bodies. Make sure you are keeping healthy foods in the house and being a good role model by what you eat as well. It takes a lot of work to be a healthy eater, but once your teen establishes healthy eating habits, it will become a natural part of her life.

35
Building self-esteem

Self-esteem is one of the keys to successfully handling stress. Adolescents with high self-esteem feel more confident about overcoming the challenges they face. They have greater faith in their abilities and are less likely to give up when obstacles are thrown in their way. As parents, it is our job to help foster our children's self-esteem. Contributing to their self-esteem is not something that simply happens overnight—we have influenced it since they were toddlers.

There are several ways you can help boost your teenager's self-esteem. Sincere words of encouragement will help. I say "sincere" because your teen has to know that you mean it. A half-hearted "You can do it" isn't going to accomplish much. It is important to praise your teenager for her accomplishments, as well as for the effort that she has made.

Conveying how proud you are of your teen's efforts and successes goes a long way in helping her build and maintain high self-esteem.

Unless your teenager is extremely gifted, chances are he is not going to succeed at everything. That is why it is important to praise effort. It is also important to provide realistic feedback to your teen. Being an "ultimate cheerleader" who ignores reality is not a way to help build self-esteem. If your teen does something wrong or fails to accomplish a goal, be realistic in discussing what went wrong. You can be realistic and do it in a positive manner.

Setbacks are also great learning experiences. Focus on what your teenager can do to overcome the problem in the future instead of dwelling on the past. It is also important to avoid, or minimize, criticism. Constructive criticism is fine, but any type of criticism that involves blame or negative comments is going to hurt your teenager's self-esteem and induce stress.

Another way to help your teenager build her self-esteem is to correct any negative or inaccurate thoughts. If your teen says she is no good at something, it is important to state that practice and effort can help improve her skills. If your teenager believes he is a bad person, it is important to point out why that is not true.

The Substance Abuse and Mental Health Services Administration, part of the U.S. Department of Health and Human Services, lists several activities that you can have your teenagers do to help build self-esteem. For example, have your teen write at least five things that she admires about herself. Have her list five of her personal strengths. Let her make a list of her five greatest achievements and a list of twenty accomplishments. The point here is to have your teen identify her strengths; by writing them down, there is visual "proof."

Another suggestion put forth by SAMHSA is to create a "celebratory scrapbook." The agency believes this is another way for your teenager to identify all of his positive features and experiences. I suggest taking it a step further and creating a scrapbook to give to your teen. It shows how much you care about your teenager while highlighting his great strengths, experiences, and accomplishments.

Another suggestion is for your teen to avoid being around negative people. Negativity drains the energy out of people and can cause others to feel down or begin viewing things from a negative perspective as well. Try to have your teenager stay around positive people, and encourage your teen to invite those friends to come over or participate in activities with them. Being in a positive environment will help lift your teenager's mood, or at least keep it up.

36
Promoting positive thinking

So, here's the deal with this: positive thinking helps make life a lot better. I'm not talking about unrealistic thinking, such as "everything will be fine" because you'll "win the lottery." Or "life is full of roses." Bad things happen, and it is not always possible to happily walk away. However, using positive-thinking skills can help reduce the stress associated with life and negative events, such as a friend or family member dying.

Promoting positive thinking is similar to helping develop high self-esteem. You point out the positives in a situation and reinforce the fact that your teenager can overcome a problem. You should be realistic but positive nonetheless.

Another aspect of promoting positive thinking is having your teenager take responsibility for his emotions. If you look at various religious, psychological, and self-help writings, you'll notice that one common theme is taking responsibility for what happens in your life. This includes learning to control your emotions instead of them having control over you. This philosophy extends to teenagers. In fact, the sooner they can learn this in life, the happier and more productive they will be.

Using affirmations

There are a few ways to develop positive thinking. One is to use affirmations. Affirmations are statements you make about yourself that reinforce positive thinking. For example, saying, "I handle stressful situations gracefully" or "I believe in my ability to overcome problems" can help your teenagers cope with stress. The key to using affirmations is to repeat them several times every day until they become part of your teen's personality. Repetition is good.

Another technique that can help reinforce affirmations is to smile while saying them. Also, thinking of something positive while saying them will equate good feelings with the statements. Affirmations don't have to be verbalized; they can be said silently. Some people write out affirmations. (This reminds me of being punished as a child, when I would have to write out the same sentence 100 times, such as "I'll never do that again.") Writing may work for your teen, or it may not.

Avoiding negativity

One thing to avoid when making affirmations is negative wording; for example, "I will not get mad when dealing with a problem." Affirmations with negative wording such as "not" do not work. Affirmations should always be stated in positive terms. As an example, rewriting the prior affirmation might look like this: "I will remain calm when dealing with a problem."

Another way to promote positive thinking is to have your teenager make a list of all the good things in her life. And then she should look at that list right after waking up in the morning. Such a list will help your teenager appreciate the positives in life. This in turn can help buffer the impact of stress.

Building on the use of affirmations and creating positive lists, your teenager should try to avoid using negative words and thoughts. Even when dealing with stressful situations, he should use positive, or at least neutral, thinking. One technique to do this is called a "mental diet." In his best-selling book *Awaken the Giant Within,* Anthony Robbins presents the mental diet, which he learned about by reading a piece by Emmet Fox, who published *The Seven Day Mental Diet* back in 1935. (If you do an Internet search on "Emmet Fox" or "mental diet," you'll find plenty of material that discusses his work.) The goal of a mental diet is to go a certain amount of time without having negative or destructive thoughts. By taking control over your thoughts, you are in a better position to deal with stress, stay positive, and focus on solving problems instead of dwelling on them.

Robbins suggests going on a ten-day mental diet. The goal is to go ten days without dwelling on "unresourceful" thoughts or feelings. When problems do arise, the focus should be on solutions. If a person starts dwelling on these negative thoughts or feelings at any point during the ten days, the whole process starts over. This is continued until a person goes the full ten days without dwelling on anything negative.

It's definitely possible to accomplish the mental diet. However, if you are going to present this option to your teenager, it might be better to gradually build up this type of thinking. Have your teen go for an hour without having a negative thought. If a negative thought pops up, she has to start over again and go for another hour. Once that is accomplished, the next challenge is to go two hours without any negative thoughts. Once again, if a negative thought appears at any time during the two-hour period, then your teenager will have to start over.

After going two hours without a negative thought, try for three or four hours, and keep increasing it until your teen can go all day avoiding negative thoughts. Now, this is not the easiest task to accomplish. In fact, it'll probably be more difficult than many food diets. However, with constant practice, your teenager will develop a stronger and healthier outlook on life and its obstacles.

37
Teaching conflict resolution skills

We all have to deal with conflict, whether minor disagreements or life-altering problems. Conflict is a daily part of life and can be especially stressful for teenagers. Many teens feel that fighting is the only acceptable way to deal with a problem. The National Youth Violence Prevention Resource Center indicates that 41 percent of teenagers would engage in a fight if challenged, while 21 percent said that walking away from a fight was a sign of weakness. One of the best things you can do to remedy these problems is help your teen learn conflict resolution techniques.

Conflict resolution isn't a touchy-feely approach to problem-solving that leaves everyone hugging and singing together. In fact, someone skilled at conflict resolution can resolve a problem without the other party even realizing the tactics that were used. Conflict resolution requires solid communication skills—the ability to listen carefully and speak clearly and calmly. The goal of conflict resolution is to have all parties obtain a better understanding of the problems at hand and develop an acceptable compromise to solve them. That means listening to each other's point of view and being civil about the problems. There also has to be a willingness to work things out.

It is that last part that can be problematic for teenagers. Teenagers may not want to work things out and just "deal with it," which may involve the threat or use of violence. And let's face it—there are going to be instances where your teen will have to just walk away or defend himself. That's an unfortunate reality and not always an easy choice to make.

Depending on the problem, it might not be possible for all parties to come to a mutual resolution. For example, disagreements between adults and teenagers may not lend themselves to compromise. Ultimately, it is the decision of the parent, teacher, or other authority figure that may have to be followed. That does not mean that your teen's conflict resolution tactics are useless. The discussions can be more civil if each party listens to the other and understands the other's position.

The most important aspect of conflict resolution is listening to the other person. It is important for your teen to listen to what the other person has to say without interrupting, displaying irritation, or becoming rude. The goal of closely listening is to be able to better appreciate the other person's perspective. It does not mean your teenager has to agree with that perspective. It simply means being polite enough to develop a better understanding. This understanding is central to developing a solution to the problem.

Working together to develop a solution is another key to conflict resolution. This ultimately means compromising so that all parties involved walk away in a better position. As I stated above, this might not always be possible for your teenager, particularly when the conflict is with an authority figure. However, conflicts with friends and peers can be negotiated in a way that reduces the level of stress associated with the problem.

38
Creating a healthy home environment

This piece of advice does not require a great deal of explanation but is often easier said than done. If your home is characterized by conflict or abuse, that needs to change. What is the cause of the conflict? Is it between you and your spouse or significant other? You and your teenager? The general environment?

If physical or verbal abuse is present, you need to seek out professional help. Unfortunately, that might involve leaving an abusive spouse, which can be emotionally, physically, and financially devastating. This is such a complex process that the only suggestion I can offer is to talk with professionals. They can assess your situation and help determine the best course of action. Regardless of the action taken, be sure that it includes counseling for you and your children.

If you drink or smoke, try to quit. As we'll discuss in the next chapter, modeling good behavior is an excellent way to help your teenager learn good habits. Removing alcohol and tobacco from the home will create a better environment and prevent future stress. The same can be said about swearing and being negative. Negativity spreads easily and quickly, and it doesn't help stress levels either. Try to be more positive by observing your actions and words and reducing stress in your own life.

39
Modeling appropriate behavior

This is another one of those suggestions that requires you to do all of the work—the "monkey see, monkey do" part of stress management. Parents are role models. As your children grow up, they see how you handle stress. If you get mad or drink or smoke or swear when dealing with problems, there's an increased chance that your kids will do the same thing when confronted with problems. They are modeling their behavior after you. You may have heard that children who grow up in abusive homes are much more likely to be abusive in their adult relationships. That's true. There are many reasons for this; however, the one that is important here is that the behavior is learned.

You will need to assess your own stress management skills if you are going to pursue this option. This means taking an objective look. You may want to ask friends and family for their input. Based on all of this, make a decision as to what you can improve. The hard part is going through with it—breaking old habits can be difficult.

If you decide to make some changes, talk to your teenager about them. Don't simply start engaging in different behavior and expect your teen to follow along. You need to explain why you are making changes and why the old ways are not effective. Otherwise, you are taking the "do as I say, not as I do" approach, which doesn't tend to be the most effective approach to use.

40
Encouraging hobbies

Does your teenager have any hobbies? If so, encourage them. Hobbies are a great way to help relieve stress. They help distract the mind, can feel good with the sense of accomplishment obtained, and promote relaxation. Having said that, I am not talking about violent video games. They may distract the mind; however, they don't promote relaxation—if anything, they can result in the opposite effect. Plus, relying on simulated (or real) violence to deal with stress isn't healthy.

There are plenty of hobbies that your teenager can pursue: model building, model railroads, scrapbooking, photography, reading, writing, cooking, cars, sports, and so forth. Pretty much anything can be a hobby, but it should be enjoyable. Otherwise, is it really a hobby?

As with other suggestions, don't force your teenager to pursue a hobby. It has to be their choice, or it'll just create more stress and irritation for your teen. Simply ask if there are any hobbies that she wants to pursue, or maybe she could resume some prior hobbies. Plus, you should have some ideas as to what your teenager likes to do. Simply see whether you can persuade her to do something that helps relieve stress.

41
Encouraging exercise

It has been known for a long time that exercise is one of the best ways to help reduce anxiety and depression. The National Institutes of Health states that twenty minutes of exercise every day can help reduce stress levels. It can also increase a person's confidence. The Centers for Disease Control and Prevention (CDC) states that children and adolescents should exercise for at least sixty minutes a day. Running, swimming, hiking, walking, and bicycling are all great forms of exercise. If your teenager is involved in sports, all the better. Encourage her to participate in activities she enjoys.

One way I like to exercise in the summers is to use an old-fashioned lawn mower. Not a riding mower, not even a push mower with a motorized blade—an old-fashioned manual lawn mower where pushing it forward makes the blade turn. It takes more effort to do and helps keep the lawn looking nice. If you're an environmentalist, it's also better for the environment since no gas or oil is needed for it to work.

Although the following is not exercise as we would think of it, it has been shown to reduce stress levels. What is it? Chewing gum. Yes, you read right. A recent study found that chewing gum can help reduce negative moods.[i] The authors have some ideas as to why this works. First, the flavor of the gum may help a person's mood; something that tastes good is enjoyable. Doing something enjoyable—chewing gum— improves a person's mood. Another possible reason is that the "effort" needed to chew gum helps reduce the chemicals in the body related to stress. Stress causes a person to release a variety of hormones into the body, which it uses to help confront the stressor. Exercise helps the body reduce the amount of hormones that are present. Since chewing gum requires some physical effort (granted, not much effort), the act of chewing helps reduce the hormone levels.

Exercise is also a form of distraction. While a person is exercising, the focus is on the body's actions, so it becomes more difficult to stew over problems and worry. More in- tense exercise, or playing a sport, requires even more con- centration. I used to walk to help relieve stress. However, that didn't actually work for me because while walking, I spent time thinking about problems. At the end of the walk, I felt more agitated than when I started! Once I switched to biking, that problem disappeared. I had to focus more on what I was doing and my surroundings. Because I was going faster, I had to pay more attention than when I walked.

If you are going to promote exercise, do it with caution. This is especially true if your teenager has an eating disorder or a poor body image. If your teenager hears you saying that she needs to exercise, negative thoughts will start popping up. *Does my own mother think I'm fat? I guess I really need to lose weight. Am I ugly?* And so on. You can stand there and explain all of the benefits of exercising, but that may not be enough. Depending on the severity of stress and how your teenager is coping, you may want to talk with a counselor before approaching your teenager about exercise. Telling someone that exercise helps with stress seems innocent enough, but to a teenager coping with stress and a possible depressive or anxiety disorder, that innocent remark can be taken the wrong way. In turn, that can make matters worse.

Another word of caution is in order. Some teenagers with body image issues will take exercise to an extreme in order to lose too much weight. I know someone who used to exercise to the point of collapsing for that very reason. If your child is involved in sports, talk with the coach to see how much exercise is warranted. If your teenager exercises but doesn't play a sport, talk to the gym teacher or a physical trainer to see what's normal. This information can help you monitor your teen's behavior and see whether exercise is being taken to an extreme.

42
Volunteering

Another suggestion to help your teenager relieve stress is to have her volunteer for a local organization. If your teen loves animals, let her volunteer to do work at a local animal shelter. If he loves helping people, he can volunteer to help at hospitals, nursing homes, or assisted-living centers. Many residents living in retirement centers or nursing homes do not receive visits from many people. It can be a heartwarming experience for your teen and the residents to just sit down and talk with some of them.

How volunteering can help reduce stress

Being a volunteer can help your teen deal with stress in a few ways. First, it can provide a distraction from stressful life events. As I've mentioned elsewhere, a distraction (especially a healthy one like volunteering) allows your teen to get a temporary break from problems. It won't solve the problems, but it will help delay them or prevent emotional burnout. Second, volunteering helps people feel better about themselves. It improves self-esteem and demonstrates they can make a positive difference in the lives of others. Further, it can help put life's problems into perspective. Helping children or adults with serious illnesses can be a wake-up call of sorts; what those with illnesses endure just to get through the day can make most of our problems look trivial.

43
Helping with learning and study strategies

Even though we are taught otherwise, not everyone learns in the same manner. Some people learn best by reading, others by listening, and others by doing. Unfortunately, our educational system is dominated by a tradition of teachers lecturing and students listening and taking notes. That approach does not work for everyone, and many students needlessly struggle because their way of learning doesn't fit in with this strategy.

What to do for your struggling teen

If your teenager is struggling with school, ask why. Maybe the courses are boring, or the material is interesting but the teacher is boring. Or your teenager is having trouble "getting it." If your teenager is struggling, one of the best things you can do is to get some help. Tutoring is a good idea. These days it is pretty easy to find tutors, especially if you're willing to work online. College students and even teachers will tutor to earn extra cash. Your teen's teachers might even be willing to devote additional time to tutoring. However, if your teenager does not like the teacher, then I don't recommend your child work with that person.

Another option is to find a local learning center. There are hundreds of centers around the country. Nationally known organizations such as Sylvan and Huntington provide excellent services. There are also countless local centers that you may be able to approach for help. These organizations help students develop effective study skills that play to their strengths. They can also help your teen work to strengthen any weaknesses.

Affording help for your teen

The key problem with tutoring or working with many learning centers is the cost. If cost is a problem, then see whether you qualify for any funding. Social workers, schools, and learning centers can help you with this.

Another option is to help your teenager learn about different study skills. There are books and Web sites that teach people to read, comprehend, and study more effectively. One of the best things (in my opinion) that you can do is have your teenager learn "mind-mapping" techniques.

Mind maps involve drawing out concepts using different colors. Mind maps look like extensive graphs—concepts can be connected to each other with lines, circles, arrows, and so on. There are several reasons this approach works, but two in particular stand out. First, using different colors for different concepts is more engaging and memorable. Let's face it—black and white can be boring. Second, taking notes and studying them can also be boring. Many people struggle to learn when they have to rely on the written word alone. Mind mapping allows people to find creative ways to highlight and illustrate key concepts. Developing and reviewing mind maps is more engaging and can be more enjoyable. These maps can also help tap the creative powers of your teenager.

I should point out that nothing I write here will adequately do justice to the power of mind mapping. I strongly recommend you do an Internet search to learn more about this study technique. There are also a few books on the subject. The one I highly recommend is *The Mind Map Book: How to Use Radiant Thinking to Maximize Your Brain's Untapped Potential* by Tony Buzan.

44
Adjusting parenting style

Your approach to parenting should also be considered a way to reduce your teen's stress. As parents, we (hopefully) want to do our best for our children. As tough as it may be, that also involves evaluating how we do things. And let's face it, no parent likes being told by someone else how to be a good parent. After all, you know your child best—how arrogant is it for someone else to butt in?

Since you're reading this book, however, you are at least somewhat open to seeing whether you should consider tweaking your approach. Therefore, I'm going to give you some useful suggestions.

Parent-teen relationship quality

One aspect of parenting is the quality of the relationship you have with your kids. Are you close? Always arguing? Distant? Trusting? Obviously, the quality of your relationship is going to have an impact on how you parent. As it relates to stress and helping your teenager, the better the relationship, the more you'll be able to help. Plus, the less conflict there is in the home, the less stress your teen will experience.

Parenting styles

It's been repeatedly shown in research that parenting style has a significant influence on children and teenagers. There are four parenting styles identified back in the 1970s by psychologist Diana Baumrind. They are authoritarian, authoritative, permissive, and uninvolved.

Authoritarian parenting style

Authoritarian parenting is pretty self-explanatory. You are the authority figure, and your children will follow your rules. Period. End of discussion. If the rules are broken, your kids will be punished. Another feature is that authoritarian parents won't explain their actions. The phrase "because I said so" is a common response when dealing with their kids' questions. The goal is to create obedient children who need no explanation. In my opinion, this is when problems crop up. I equate authoritarian parenting with someone running a military boot camp, where fear of punishment is the "great motivator." Children of authoritarian parents are less happy and have lower levels of self-esteem compared to children of authoritative parents. It makes sense: What is a child really learning from this style of parenting? It's one thing to be an authority figure and enforce the rules. All parents should do that. However, there are always learning opportunities when children break the rules and parents need to explain them.

Instead of telling them to do what you say "because you said so," it's better to explain why. Understanding why something should be done or avoided may reduce the likelihood of your child doing it again. Of course, if your teenager has some form of conduct disorder, you'll need to work with his doctors to develop the right style of parenting. This may include using an authoritarian approach.

Authoritative parenting style

Another parenting style is the authoritative style. This type of parenting style involves being an authority figure and establishing rules. Consequences are also in place for when the rules are broken. However, the big difference is how the rules are conveyed. Instead of using a "because-I-said-so" approach, authoritative parents take the time to explain why the rules are in place. They also are not as punitive when dealing with consequences. Children can also have some input. Authoritative parents are willing to listen and make compromises at times. Ultimately, the parents have the final say, but allowing the children to have input helps build a trusting relationship. I like to think of this style as a flexible and more supportive form of authoritarian parenting.

Permissive parenting style

Permissive parenting is a style that does more long-term harm than good. Permissive parents do not like confrontation and typically do not make many demands on their children. Consequences are almost nonexistent, and the parents act more like friends than parents. However, children and teenagers need authority figures in their lives. Parents are responsible for instilling self-control and a sense of right and wrong in their children. Minimizing the authority aspect of parenting may help reduce parent-child conflicts, but it will create more problems down the road. Children and teens will be less likely to worry about the consequences of their behavior since they were rarely punished earlier in life. They may rebel against authority figures, such as teachers, since they did not have to deal with authority at home.

Being supportive and using open communication is great. Not being an authority figure—well, that's not so great.

Uninvolved parenting style

The last, and worst, parenting style is uninvolved parenting. The name says it all: these parents do not take much of a role in their children's lives. Uninvolved parents may provide the basic necessities—food, clothing, and shelter.

But they do not pay much attention to their children. You can think of it as growing up without having parents. These parents often make it clear they do not care about their children. Actions may speak louder than words, but words like "I don't care" can also hurt. How is a child supposed to develop self-control and self-esteem when his own parents can't be bothered with him? Children of uninvolved parents will, on average, have the most problematic behaviors and difficulties in life.

Is it too late for change?

If the relationship you have with your teenager is negative, simply changing it will not immediately work. Unfortunately, depending on what has gone on in the past, combined with the age of your child, changing your style may not work at all. By the time your child has reached the late teenage years, your influence has significantly weakened. Nevertheless, there still may be some changes you can effectively make.

Improving your style

Which type of parent are you? I assume you're not an uninvolved parent—if you were, then why would you be reading this book? Maybe you're an authoritarian parent. The best advice I can give is to loosen up a little and develop more of a two-way relationship with your teenager. Are you a permissive parent? You're going to have to enforce more rules. That's not going to be the easiest thing in the world to do if you've given your children too much leeway in the past. That'll lead to some level of rebellion against you, but keep in mind the positive outcome of your efforts.

If the relationship you have with your teenager isn't good, talk to a counselor. Do some Internet research on parenting skills. Go to the local bookstore and look for parenting books. Believe me, you'll find plenty of books that cover every aspect of parenting, including ones you've never thought of. If you are serious about trying to adjust your parenting style, keep this in mind: try to leave your ego out of it. Your goal is to find ways to help your teenager manage stress, even if that means evaluating how you do things. Which is more important: helping your teen, or believing your way is the right way?

45
Teaching time-management skills

As I've discussed in previous chapters, school can be a significant source of stress. Between school, home, sports, and work, your teenager may struggle to get everything done. That can be even more difficult if your teen has problems managing time. The easiest way to help deal with this is to help him learn time-management skills. Using time-management skills has been shown to reduce anxiety and stress. And they're pretty easy to implement.

You may have seen a newspaper story or news broadcast that gives you tips on how to save money. You know, pay attention to the little things that add up. Don't buy coffee every morning. Bring your lunch, share a ride, make a grocery list and stick to it, and so forth. Well, the same principle applies to time management. The little breaks and distractions can add up to a good chunk of time.

Homework on the computer

If your teenager uses the computer a lot for homework, have him keep the e-mail program closed. If he's writing a paper and already has his research collected, keep the Web browser closed. If your teenager loves using an instant messaging program or Facebook, definitely keep that off! That can be the equivalent of trying to study while at a friend's party—it might happen, but I wouldn't count on it. This is part of a concept known as creating a dedicated, distraction-free space to get work done. Ideally, your teenager will be free of other distractions as well. If it's not possible for him to be isolated, at least try to keep his computer distractions to a minimum (or eliminate them).

A very simple suggestion is to block out chunks of time for each task. For example, set aside an hour (or two) for homework, and make it the only thing to be done during that period. If your child gets distracted after a certain amount of time, block out periods that do not exceed that time. For example, let's say your son gets antsy and distracted after studying for thirty minutes. Then he should not block out a time for more than thirty minutes. This may mean he needs to block out several thirty-minute periods during a day to get the homework done. Between those periods, other blocks of time are set aside to do other tasks, such as chores.

A key aspect of time management is prioritizing work. Have your teenager outline the tasks that need to be accomplished. What are the due dates? Which are the most important? What tasks need to be done now or can wait until later? Based on this information, he can determine the order in which tasks should be completed. By doing this, your teenager starts with the end in mind. In other words, by looking at the final outcome of each task and then prioritizing the tasks, your teenager is working backwards to develop a strategy.

Stephen Covey, in his book *The 7 Habits of Highly Effective People,* discusses time-management strategies and how to prioritize work. Sean Covey's *The 7 Habits of Highly Effective Teens* deals with similar matters but is obviously geared toward teenagers. Both Steven's and Sean's works go into a lot more detail, but working backwards to strategize is their basic idea behind prioritizing work. Their books and workbooks are definitely worth reading for more information.

To help your teenager do all of this, invest in a planner for him. It doesn't have to be an expensive or fancy one, just something basic that has a calendar with daily, weekly, and monthly options. This will allow your teen to see what needs to be done on a given day, and provides an overview of the week's tasks and a broad look at the upcoming month. There are plenty of computer programs that can also be used for planning. However, if your teenager is easily distracted on the computer, it may be better to use the old-fashioned paper and pencil.

46
Using humor

The last suggestion for you to help your teen reduce stress is to use humor when you feel it is appropriate. Laughing and smiling are two of the easiest ways to help improve mood. You can help those reactions surface by using humor, so use it when possible.

Don't push the humor if your teenager simply isn't in the mood for it. You should be able to tell by the reaction your comments receive. Trying too hard to make the situation better can actually backfire. If your teenager is seriously depressed or suicidal, avoid putting on a comedy show.

That being said, there are no formulas or guidelines to follow when trying to lighten the mood. You have to assess the situation and try, to the best of your ability, to understand what your teenager is going through. For the average stressful day, lighthearted comments are usually good to help keep the mood light and lessen your teen's stress.

References

Chapter 1: Peer pressure

i. Allen, J. P., Porter, M. R., & McFarland, F. C. (2006). Leaders and followers in adolescent close friendships: Susceptibility to peer influence as a predictor of risky behavior, friendship instability, and depression. *Development and Psychopathology, 18,* 155-172.

ii. Renna, F., Grafova, I. B., & Thakur, N. (2008). The effect of friends on adolescent body weight. *Economics and Human Biology, 6,* 377-387.

iii. Shomaker, L. B., & Furman, W. (2009). Interpersonal

influence on late adolescent girls' and boys' disordered eating. *Eating Behaviors, 10,* 97-106.

Chapter 2: Low self-esteem

i. March of Dimes. *Youth Health Education Series: Self-esteem, peer pressure, & stress management.* Retrieved April 10, 2010, from www.marchofdimesyouth.com/tools/guide/esteem.pdf.

ii. Reasoner, Robert. The true meaning of self-esteem. *National Association for Self-Esteem.* Retrieved April 10, 2010, from http://www.self-esteem-nase.org/what.php.

iii. Martyn-Nemeth, P., Penckofer, S., Gulanick, M., Velsor-Friedrich, B., & Bryant, F. B. (2009). The Relationships Among Self-Esteem, Stress, Coping, Eating Behavior, and Depressive Mood in Adolescents. *Research in Nursing & Health, 32,* 96-109.

iv. Boden, J. M., Fergusson, D. M., & Horwood, L. J. (2008). Does adolescent self-esteem predict later life outcomes? A test of the causal role of self-esteem. *Development and Psychology, 20,* 319-339.

Chapter 3: School

i. Suldo, S. M., Shaunessy, E., & Hardesty, R. (2008). Relationships Among Stress, Coping, and Mental Health in

High-Achieving High School Students. *Psychology in the Schools, 45,* 273-290.

ii. Dinkes, R., Kemp, J., & Baum, K. (2009). *Indicators of School Crime and Safety: 2009* (NCES 2010–012/ NCJ 228478). National Center for Education Statistics, Institute of Education Sciences, U.S. Department of Education, and Bureau of Justice Statistics, Office of Justice Programs, U.S. Department of Justice. Washington, D.C.

Chapter 8: Friends and dating

i. The American Bar Association. *National Teen Dating Violence Prevention Initiative: Teen Dating Violence Facts.* Retrieved from http://www.abanet.org/unmet/teendating/facts.pdf.

Chapter 9: Puberty

i. Ge, X., Conger, R. D., & Elder, J. H., Jr. (1996). Coming of Age Too Early: Pubertal Influences on Girls' Vulnerability to Psychological Distress. *Child Development, 67,* 3386-3400.

ii. Conley, C. S., & Rudolph, K. D. (2009). The emerging sex difference in adolescent depression: Interacting contributions of puberty and peer stress. *Development and Psychopathology, 21,* 593-620.

iii. Westling, E., Andrews, J. A., Hampson, S. E., & Peterson, M. (2008). Pubertal Timing and Substance Use: The Effects of Gender, Parental monitoring and deviant peers. *Journal of Adolescent Health, 42,* 555-563.

Chapter 10: Sex and sexuality

i. Almeida, J., Johnson, R. M., Corliss, H. L., Molnar, B. E., & Azrael, D. (2009). Emotional Distress Among LGBT Youth: The Influence of Perceived Discrimination Based on Sexual Orientation. *Journal of Youth and Adolescence, 38,* 1001-1014.

ii. Jiang, Y., Perry, D. K., & Hesser, J. E. (2010). Adolescent Suicide and Health Risk Behaviors: Rhode Island's 2007 Youth Risk Behavior Survey. *American Journal of Preventative Medicine, 38,* 551-555.

Chapter 15: Alcohol use

i. Substance Abuse and Mental Health Services Administration. (2009). *Results from the 2008 National Survey on Drug Use and Health: National Findings* (Office of Applied Studies, NSDUH Series H-36, HHS Publication No. SMA 09-4434). Rockville, MD.

Chapter 19: Nonlethal self-injury

i. Lloyd-Richardson, E. E., Perrine, N., Dierker, L., & Kelley, M. L. (2007). Characteristics and functions of non-suicidal self-injury in a community sample of adolescents. *Psychological Medicine, 37,* 1183-1192.

ii. Hasking, P., Momeni, R., Swannell, S., & Chia, S. (2008). The Nature and Extent of Non-Suicidal Self-Injury in a Non-Clinical Sample of Young Adults. *Archives of Suicide Research, 12,* 208-218.

iii. Kerr, P. L., Muehlenkamp, J. J., & Turner, J. M. (2010). Nonsuicidal Self-injury: A Review of Current Research for Family Medicine and Primary Care Physicians. *Journal of the American Board of Family Medicine, 23,* 240-259.

Chapter 23: Sleep patterns

i. Dahl, R. E., & Lewin, D. S. (2002). Pathways to Adolescent Health: Sleep Regulation and Behavior. *Journal of Adolescent Health, 31,* 175-184.

Chapter 24: Eating patterns

i. Felton, J., Cole, D.A., Tilghman-Osborne, C., & Maxwell, M. A. (2010). The relation of weight change to depressive symptoms in adolescence. *Development and Psychopathology, 23,* 205-216.

ii. Nguyen-Rodriguez, S. T., Unger, J. B., & Spruijt-Metz, D. (2009). Psychological determinants of Emotional Eating in Adolescents. *Eating Disorders, 17,* 211-224.

Chapter 41: Encouraging exercise

i. Scholey, A., Haskall, C., Robertson, B., Kennedy, D., Milne, A., & Wetherell, M. (2009). Chewing gum alleviates negative mood and reduces cortisol during acute laboratory psychological stress. *Physiology & Behavior, 97,* 304-312.